GOOD FOOD

Fruits

Julia Adams

PowerKiDS
press.
New York

Published in 2011 by The Rosen Publishing Group Inc.
29 East 21st Street, New York, NY 10010

First Edition

Editor: Julia Adams
Managing Editor: Victoria Brooker
Designer: Paul Cherrill
Picture Researcher: Julia Adams
Food and Nutrition Consultant: Ester Davies
Photo Models: Asha Francis, Lydia Washbourne

Library of Congress Cataloguing-in-Publication Data

Adams, Julia, 1979-
Fruits / by Julia Adams. -- 1st ed.
    p. cm. -- (Good food)
Includes index.
ISBN 978-1-4488-3271-2 (library binding)
1. Fruit--Juvenile literature. I. Title. II. Series: Adams, Julia,
1979- Good food.
SB357.2.A33 2011
634--dc22
                            2010023708

Photographs:
Alamy: Spyros Bourboulis 1/9, Ed Young 10, Mick Rock 11,
Helen Sessions 15; Andy Crawford: 2, 13, 16, 20, 22, 23;
iStock: monkeybusinessimages 4, ktaylorg 19/OFC;
Shutterstock: Kruchankova Maya 5, Dino O. 6,
shalunishka 7, karnizz 8, Marta P. 12, Hannamariah 14,
Monkey Business Images 17, Feng Yu 18, Gelpi 21.

Manufactured in China
CPSIA Compliance Information: Batch #WAW1102PK: For Further Information
contact Rosen Publishing, New York, New York at 1-800-237-9932

Web Sites

Due to the changing nature of Internet
links, PowerKids Press has developed
an online list of Web sites related to
the subject of this book. This site is
updated regularly. Please use this link
to access this list:
http://www.powerkidslinks.com/gf/fruits

Contents

Good for You

Everyone needs to eat the right kind of food to stay healthy. The food we cook and eat comes from plants and animals.

Fresh food, such as vegetables, fruit, and grains, can be eaten in many ways.

Fruit is good for us because it has vitamins and minerals. Our bodies need these to keep the heart healthy, and to help us stop catching colds.

Eating lots of fresh fruit and vegetables is good for you.

There are many different kinds of fruit. How many do you know?

What Is Fruit?

Apples, bananas, and oranges are all fruit. They come from plants. Fruit can be many shapes, sizes, and colors.

Can you name all the fruits in this picture?

We eat the flesh of a fruit. The flesh can be soft or hard. It is often sweet and juicy. We can eat the skin of some fruits, too.

You need to peel the skin off a banana before you eat it!

How Fruit Grows

Fruit grows on many different kinds
of plants. It grows on trees and bushes.
In the spring, these plants grow flowers.
The flowers are called blossoms.

This apple tree is covered in blossoms.

After the blossoms fall off, the fruit begins to grow. When the fruit is ripe, it is ready to pick and eat.

Apples can be red, green, yellow, or brown.

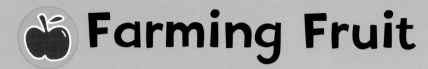 Farming Fruit

Most of the fruit that we eat is grown on farms. Farmers grow the fruit plants in rows. This makes it easier to pick the fruit when it is ripe.

These are rows of grapevines.

The ripe fruit is picked by hand or by a machine. Then the fruit is packed into boxes and taken to stores.

These grapes have just been picked.

Citrus Fruits

Oranges, grapefruit, and lemons are all citrus fruits. They grow on trees in hot countries.

Lemons are green at first. They are ripe when they turn yellow.

Citrus fruits have a thick, shiny skin.
You have to peel them to eat them.
Citrus fruits are very juicy.

You can squeeze citrus fruits, such as oranges, to make fruit juice.

Try citrus fruits such as grapefruit, limes, tangerines, and lemons. What do they taste like?

Orchard Fruits

Apples, pears, nectarines, and plums are all orchard fruits. They grow on trees. Farmers grow these fruit trees on a piece of land called an orchard.

The fruit trees in an orchard are planted in rows. These are nectarine trees.

Many orchard fruits can be pressed to make fruit juices. They can also be dried to make a tasty snack.

Can you guess which dried orchard fruits these are?

Tropical Fruits

Some fruits only grow in hot places. Tropical fruits are from places that are warm and wet all year round.

How many of these tropical fruits do you know?

We often add tropical fruits to desserts. We also use them in smoothies and juices.

Tropical fruits are tasty in a fruit salad.

Did you know that bananas can be yellow, red, or purple?

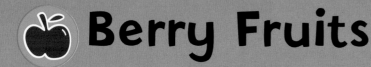

Berry Fruits

Gooseberries, strawberries, and blueberries are all berries. They grow on bushes and trees.

These blueberries grow on trees.

18

We eat berries in cereals and desserts. Some berries, such as strawberries, can also be used to make jelly.

Can you name any berries that are made into jelly?

Vegetable Fruits

Tomatoes, cucumbers, pumpkins, and peppers are called vegetable fruits. This is because they are not very sweet.

Vegetable fruits grow from a flower and have seeds, just like other fruit.

We use vegetable fruits in many savory dishes. We can eat them raw, or roast, bake, or fry them.

Tomatoes, cucumbers, peppers, and avocados are great in salads.

Make a Fruit Salad

Follow this recipe to make a delicious fruit salad as a snack or for breakfast.

1. Wash the apples and dry them with some paper towels.

2. Peel the banana.

3. Use the knife to chop the banana into slices. Ask an adult to help you with this. Add the slices to the bowl.

4. Ask an adult to peel the kiwi for you. Cut it in half and slice it. Add the slices to the bowl.

5. After an adult has helped you cut the apples into quarters, slice each quarter. Add the pieces to the bowl.

6. Ask an adult to cut an orange in half. Squeeze the orange over the fruit in the bowl. Mix the orange juice with the fruit. Enjoy!

Glossary and Further Information

blossom the flower of a plant

flesh the soft inside of a fruit that we eat

grapevine the plant that grapes grow on

minerals substances in food that keep our bodies healthy

ripe when a fruit or vegetable is ready to eat

seeds parts of plants that grow to form new plants

vitamins substances in food that help keep our bodies healthy and keep us from catching colds

Books

Fruit on Your Plate
by Honor Head
(Smart Apple Media, 2009)

The Fruit Group
by Mari Schuh
(Capstone Press, 2006)

Index

ML   6/11